Little Business Books

Change

Written by **Ruth Percival**

Illustrated by **Dean Gray**

Published in 2026 by Windmill Books,
an Imprint of Rosen Publishing
2544 Clinton St.
Buffalo, NY 14224

First published in Great Britain in 2024 by Hodder & Stoughton
Copyright © Hodder & Stoughton Limited, 2024

Credits
Series Editor: Amy Pimperton
Series Designer: Peter Scoulding
Consultant: Philippa Anderson
Philippa Anderson has a business degree and is a writer
and communications consultant who advises multinationals.
She authors and contributes to business books.

Cataloging-in-Publication Data

Names: Percival, Ruth, author. | Grey, Dean, illustrator.
Title: Change / Ruth Percival, illustrated by Dean Grey.
Description: Buffalo, NY : Windmill Books, 2026. | Series: Little business books | Includes glossary and index.
Identifiers: ISBN 9781725396432 (pbk.) | ISBN 9781725396449 (library bound) | ISBN 9781725396456 (ebook)
Subjects: LCSH: Change (Psychology)--Juvenile literature. | Success in business--Juvenile literature.
Classification: LCC BF637.C4 P478 2026 | DDC 158.1--dc23

All rights reserved.

All facts and statistics were up to date at the time of press.

No part of this book may be reproduced in any form without permission
in writing from the publisher, except by a reviewer.

Printed in the United States of America

CPSIA Compliance Information: Batch #CSWM26
For Further Information contact Rosen Publishing at 1-800-237-9932

Contents

4	What Is Change?
6	Get Ready for Change
8	Try New Things
10	Challenge Accepted!
12	A Better Idea
14	A New Idea
16	Learn from Others
18	Swap Around
20	Work Together
22	Be Flexible
24	A Change for the Better
26	Change Old for New
28	A Bigger Place
30	Change and You
31	Notes for Sharing This Book
32	Glossary

What Is Change?

Change is when something becomes different.

Winter changes into spring. Your body changes as you grow older. Baking changes ingredients into a cake.

Sometimes change is something you can feel. You might change your mind about something. Change can sometimes make you feel worried if you don't know what will happen next.

WHY IS CHANGE IMPORTANT?

In business, change is important. Change might mean inventing a new product, serving new customers, or moving to a bigger place.

For you, change might mean moving to a new house or being brave enough to try something for the first time.

What will our animal friends find out about change in business and about themselves?

Get Ready for Change

Everyone plays outside on warm, sunny days. Customers buy lots of bikes, kites, and footballs from Enzo Elephant's toy shop.

Enzo predicts a change. He calls the toy warehouse.

The next day, indoor toys and games arrive – along with storm clouds!

Enzo Elephant's customers are delighted. Now they have toys to play with inside while it rains outside!

Knowing change is coming helps you to be ready.

Try New Things

Pip Penguin's ice tours are AMAZING, but very expensive. Something needs to change to attract more customers.

Pip Penguin has a brilliant idea – virtual reality ice tours! They will be less expensive, but just as much fun!

Change can encourage you to try new things.

Challenge Accepted!

Customers love Peggy Polar Bear's fun snow animal statues. But Wei Wolf wants Peggy to make him a snow garden instead!

Changing her product will be a challenge, but Peggy accepts!

Peggy Polar Bear gets creative ... and makes Wei Wolf an amazing snow and ice garden.

Try to stay positive when change brings challenges.

A Better Idea

Even when wearing her best shoe design, Tilly Tiger can't beat Chip Cheetah in a race.

Tilly decides to change her shoe design to help her go faster.

Remember, some changes take time and effort to make.

A New Idea

Wei Wolf wonders why birds don't buy his caps.

It's because they blow off when we fly fast.

Wei invents a new product just for birds. Hats with chinstraps!

Learn from Others

Customers are waiting in line to get a table at Peter Panda's pizza restaurant. But he can't serve everyone – there isn't enough space.

Peter sees Kit Kangaroo zipping past, delivering cakes. This gives Peter a great idea.

Peter Panda opens a new pizza delivery service.
Now everyone can enjoy his delicious pizzas!

Learning from others can inspire you to change.

Swap Around

Kit Kangaroo's café has a problem. Pip Penguin keeps burning the cakes and Tilly Tiger has mixed up the orders – again!

"I have an idea. Let's swap your jobs."

It turns out that Tilly Tiger is an expert baker. And Pip Penguin remembers everything!

Now the café runs perfectly.

Be open to swapping things around.

Work Together

There's chaos at Kiki Koala's tree farm! Everyone is making mistakes because they aren't working as a team.

Kiki knows what needs to change.

20

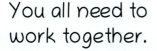

You all need to work together.

Now, instead of everyone doing jobs by themselves, they help one another with each task in turn. This simple change helps the whole team to work better together.

Change feels good when you work with others.

Be Flexible

Chip Cheetah hires Omar Owl as a yoga instructor.
But Omar keeps falling asleep in class!

22

To solve the problem, Chip Cheetah lets Omar Owl work at night.

Customers love the new night classes and Omar is happier, too.

Being flexible means you can adapt to change.

A Change for the Better

Milly Monkey wonders why her customers are grumpy when they leave her zip line adventure park. Haven't they had fun?

Milly Monkey makes a smart change. The last zip line now ends near the exit. This change makes her business more organized – and more fun.

Change can make a good thing even better.

Change Old for New

Omar Owl's kite-making machine is very old.

It keeps making a mess.

What a mess! Omar knows he must buy a new machine, or his business won't have anything to sell.

The new kite-making machine is AMAZING!
Omar Owl is glad he made a change!

When things go wrong, a change could fix the problem.

A Bigger Place

Roarsome Cars has a big problem. Leon Lion has too many cars in his tiny garage and it's putting off customers.

Leon Lion finds the perfect new garage, with lots of space for his cars!

When you outgrow things, it is a good time to make a change.

Change and You

Our animal friends have learned a lot about change in business. What they have learned can help you, too!

Tilly Tiger made her product even better. Change can help you to keep improving and learning.

Enzo Elephant was organized and prepared. Change is often easier to deal with when you know it is coming.

Chip Cheetah was flexible. When you can adapt to change, you can solve problems quickly and your confidence and resilience get stronger.

Notes for Sharing This Book

This book introduces business ideas around the topic of change, which link to core personal and social skills, such as teamwork, listening, and being fair.

Talk to the child or class about what business is and why we need good businesses. You can use each scenario to discuss change themes. For example, talk about a time when the child was inspired by others to make a positive change.

Change can sometimes feel scary, but it is important to be open to new ideas and experiences and have faith in our ability to cope with change. Talk about a time when the child experienced a change, such as starting a new school. How did they feel before and after?

Glossary

adapt to change something to use it in a new way

business a company that buys, makes, or sells goods or services to make money

chaos a mess; confusion

customer someone who buys things from a business

effort to try very hard

expert someone who is very skilled at something; someone who knows a lot about a topic

flexible able to adapt easily to changing circumstances

hire to take on someone to work for you

inspire to make someone feel like they want to do something

invent to create or design something new

predict to say or think that something will happen in the future

products the goods or services that a business makes or sells

research to look carefully into something to see what more you can learn

virtual reality a world made by a computer program that feels and sounds real to the person using it

warehouse a big building where goods are stored before they are sold